POPPY

Joseph Minden is a poet and secondary school teacher. Past publications include *Paddock calls: The Nightbook* (slub press); *The Beef Onion* with Will Harris and Hugh Foley, *Derivatives* with Kat Addis, *Woodvale* with the Beam-eye Babies and *Diptych Brian* (all from The Minutes Press); and *Soft Hans* (The Koppel Press).

Poppy

JOSEPH MINDEN

CARCANET POETRY

First published in Great Britain in 2022 by
Carcanet
Alliance House, 30 Cross Street
Manchester, M2 7AQ
www.carcanet.co.uk

A CIP catalogue record for this book is
available from the British Library.

ISBN 978 1 80017 271 5

Book design by Andrew Latimer
Printed in Great Britain by SRP Ltd, Exeter, Devon

The publisher acknowledges financial
assistance from Arts Council England.

CONTENTS

who bridges forgetfulness and memory
  —Zaffar Kunial, 'Poppy'

an effort to think against what I find in myself
  —David Scott, in conversation with Stuart Hall

THE ROLLRIGHT STONES

As I stepped out from Chipping Norton,
the tears froze on my cheeks and rimed
my eyelashes. A smashed Wordsworth
    half buried itself in snow in my brain.
    Stone eyes beamed at jaunty angles
from the earth, searchlights poked around
        among the airborne menhirs,
    the cloud samurai of Buckingham
    drifted ever more towards the west
and I walked up to meet my greatest fear:
        a circle of strangers.

    We were fenced in, you and I,
    stones fumbling into brambles,
    ghost architecture of foliage,
the fuzz of sketches, bee-distracted
        litter among mushrooms,
    Huntley & Palmers biscuit tins,
pemmican crumbling in the polar aisles,
    dog food odour, a blue flag bearing
    the heads of seven wolves arranged
    in a ring slipping from the permafrost,
the devastating arbitrariness of any
    possible exit from the circle.

    The road was visible, escaping
    over sly humps evoked as castles.
        So you smiled, but the water
    stood in your eyes. At which point
the bald hordes of Crawley Museum,
    the trumpet ghosts. On your face

the white nosebleed that goes up,
sight loss moving out from the centre,
        materialisation of the pupil.
You take my neck in your hands, speaking
        spectrally of the noose.
        The hottest day of the year.
        The hottest day of the era.
        There it is in the park,
            the circle.

    Fear is archaeological, the finds
    yielded at the Ness of Brodgar
every summer in the six week window
of sunlight that falls flat out of the sky:
Neolithic people having a singsong
among their holy oxen when the wind
        blew in. I fumble up
    a kneebone and the sod is wet,
    the picnic ended. A ripple
    of flints and potsherds indicates
aftermath, ghosts the arrangement
    of friends fallen out in a circle.

The fact of the song hangs back
but the order is in the system.
        Megalith hum,
        the mind consumed
as Didcot Power Station's last fuel,
so external, so huge, so subterranean.
    Of course the body would break
    down in the continental shadow
of such a Death Star, so suspended,
so ethereal. The quivering mind
    a beechwood under a day of rain.

I was becoming a very angry bear,
not blisters on my toes but mushrooms.
            At night, the dread
            horse in its paddock
thumped around the perimeter and
with every thud a face came on in the dark,
a stake-out of candles in the park,
known, blank and heinously inside
my own collapsing head in the tent
            beside your terrifying body.

I dreamt of a gaunt man dropping
golden washers to the ground,
        how they fell out in a circle,
five or seven friends in the grass,
how they sounded like one large,
resonant panel of struck metal.
The park flickered and the circle stood.
            Suddenly, there was
            a basin of silence
            empty and growing
dark, a couple of ghosts playing football.
Fear split into an assemblage of faces
            that could not be co-opted.

        It is my right to run away.
There is an ever-replenished downrushing
            in my heart.
    It steps out of the dark in your face
speaking tender, normal questions.
Your head is not there but your neck
        is the source of the Thames,
        your torso is by Quinlan Terry,
        your ribcage is Marble Run.
I beat time by burying the many

moving artefacts you communicate,
the light fading and terror fading with it,
dilation of the pupil.

The dark is a ring,
it is impossible to know how populous,
how many others now sit on the grass
descended from their own chest
out of fear
into love out of
proportion, the two pools of their eyes,
the entanglement of radio waves
transmitting present music
when the earth gone, not the
maintenance of things already given
over to safety without end but
the excavation of indefinite
pasts in the spirit of presence.

*

NEWHAVEN

I found a boy face down
at the mouth of a path.
The path ran off
between two fences.
His forehead rested
on his bent right forearm.
I couldn't see his face,
only his black hair,
blue jacket,
the nape of his neck,
the curve of his back,
the weeds crowding in.
Annual meadow-grass.
Mind-your-own-business.

I thought I'd better see
if this boy was OK.
So I did.
I checked in,
touching his throat
for a pulse.
Hey man, are you OK?
At this, he stirred
and looked up
surprisingly quickly.
Just resting,
he replied.
Just resting
like a dead young man.

SERRE ROAD CEMETERY NO. 2

It's so - cinematic.
    So it was.
An enormous array
    of bright stones.

A testament, a crowd,
    so managed
it was impossible
    not to, um,

become sedated. Why
    do I feel
as though I am waking
    in a dream?

I asked Jason, as we
    walked around
aimlessly above the
    body parts.

Because they had to try
    to re-fuse
what had been dismembered
    by the war:

a permanent body
    composed of
transitory parts,
    he replied.

Did my mum ever tell
    you about
uncle Roy? I asked. He
    shook his head.

          *

Visiting Ypres to imagine cemeteries, Edwin Lutyens wrote home

    a ribbon of isolated graves like a milky way across miles of
    country where men were tucked in where they fell.

          *

In the book
Where Poppies Blow
by John Lewis-Stempel,
he explains that

    in the cemeteries,
    where memory was planted,
    the French countryside
    was sequestered
    and remodelled
    to become
    little bits of Britain.

          *

In 1960
the Imperial War Graves Commission
changed its name.

*

I lost myself and found a field
    of poppies lanced for gum,
for milky, languid tears: the yield
    of soft somniferum,

and standing in the field were two
    whom poppies comforted.
It was Maria Logan who
    began to speak. She said:

    Be mine the balm, whose sov'reign pow'r
        Can still the throb of Pain;
    The produce of the scentless flow'r,
        That strews Hindostan's plain.

Then Sara Coleridge spoke up,
    compelled to talk in turn
about the nullifying cup
    that terminates concern.

    When poor Mama long restless lies,
        She drinks the poppy's juice;
    That liquor soon can close her eyes,
        And slumber soon produce:

    O then my sweet, my happy boy
        Will thank the Poppy-flower
    Which brings the sleep to dear Mama
        At midnight's darksome hour.

The poppies stretched out, row on row,
    as far as I could see
and both the women turned to go
    without noticing me.

*

In November 2010, at the Great Hall of the People in
Tiananmen Square in Beijing, Prime Minister David Cameron
and a number of other British politicians were asked to remove
Remembrance Day poppies from their lapels.

A Chinese official explained that they would cause offence as
reminders of the Opium Wars in which the British had forced
China to

A British official explained that they mean a great deal to us
and we would be wearing them all the same.

*

En route to China
in June 1840
    to act against the Chinese
an Englishman
of the HMS *Modeste*
experienced
a bittersweet
reunion.

    On the 20th the island of Penang was in sight;
    a spot that recalls to my memory many happy days; when,
    having just passed my examination for lieutenant,
    and full of hope

I gaily wandered over its verdant hills,
while day after day fled rapidly by
amidst the joyous group of my first and warmest friends.
Alas! where are they now?

*

Blow, bugles, blow! They brought us, for our dearth,
    Holiness, lacked so long, and Love, and Pain.
Honour has come back, as a king, to earth,
    And paid his subjects with a royal wage;
And Nobleness walks in our ways again;
    And we have come into our heritage.

DEPARTURE

In your Somerset, I learnt nostalgia.
    Its precise, imperial bloom
        spread from my chest like an exhalation

until the whole of England reeled with pollen
    and I was always a soldier
        dreaming of the last summer before war.

The ferry out of Newhaven was desolate,
    its interiors bleached with lemony light,
        its small lights lonely on the empty sea.

Jason and I tried to sleep. We dozed,
    two figures among the platoon of vacant chairs,
        our heads tilted back against the leather

until a ring-a-ring o'roses of pissed-up lads
    burst in from the bar with pints, slapping
        the slot machines with their free hands.

Then we began to talk. Jason knew about
    you and me, the way it had come to an end
        and how I had been found in the field,

my heart broken open to release
    all the dust motes of Glastonbury which rose in a haze,
        shaping figures dazzled as if leaving Eden,

mournful shepherds of the high Quantocks,
    well-to-do squires of the pastures of Frome,
        their forearms raised against the sudden sky.

You went to Malaysia, to George Town, Penang,
the first British settlement in Southeast Asia.
My East Indiamen set sail directly.

The lads had drained their lagers to the dregs.
It was still too dark to see but, behind us,
England slipped out of eyeshot.

UNION JACK

The red parts
of the field
are the bloody
and forgetful

poppy tongues.
The blue parts
are Picardy's
forgotten cornflowers.

*

[

]

DAWN TWILIGHT

Now
the road
out of the sea
the verges
low
peeling back
whipping past
peopled with
frozen eyes

someone always
about to step out
out of the grasses
out of the
bottomless field
out of the
thought of it
into the light
and go up

HISTORIOGRAPHY

Jason taught me everything I know about history. Once, we were at an Albrecht Dürer exhibition: one drawing was haunted by the lines of another. Jason explained how, not having rubbers, draughtsmen such as Dürer would take a sponge and wipe away, imperfectly, the form they wanted to replace; how a trace remained.

Jason moved on to another part of the exhibition and I walked round to the other side of the case to discover that this wasn't true. There was simply another drawing on the reverse side of the paper. I can't remember what either of the drawings were.

PICARDY

Having travelled
all night we pulled
over for a nap
in dappled shade

twenty minutes'
sleep a light so
yellow the green
was almost bleached

articulate
in the wind and
out of the white
chalk of the downs

blossoms hawkweed
knapweed purple
vetch pimpernel
campanulas

blue chicory
yellow ragwort
white yarrow and
camomile and

oats barley wheat
and when we woke
we could have been
in Sussex or

AMIENS

Everything had a limey pallor.
It was too cold for my summer jacket.
There wasn't a single cafe open,
not even one selling yesterday's
stale breakfast. We were in the market
for anything. I sprawled on a bench
in the Place Notre Dame
beneath the many faces
of the cathedral's west face.
Jason blew on his hands.

The first woman of the morning
appeared at the corner of the square
and grew until, life-size, she passed,
her expression resolute,
her features visibly carved,
her departure marked
by a pigeon explosion.
Dawn came like stone,
lightened and lightened
the many faces.

FANG

How many
in the mass
grave? I asked
my teacher
at Deutscher
Soldatenfriedhof

Langemark,
the pit dark,
clouded with
grey-green
bursts, mute,
complete but

*

forced apart
about thousands –
but *thousands* –
of minute, bone-
bright places
in its body.

Tall, white
and slender,
he fell to
the floor,
two red holes
in his neck.

NOSFERATU

Odours are how
interiors make themselves
known to the world.
My father lost his sense of smell
when, or was it because,
he stepped onto the sea
at Horumersiel-Schellig,
beliebter Ferienort,
which is near Wangerland,
and it was so frozen
nothing could be smelt.
The sea and the sky,
which went on for ever,
hummed like a freezer,
and underneath was a body
of water, alive and populated,
over which the creaking of his steps
extended like shadows of fingers
across the lawn in the park
on a summer's day.
Long fingers,
much longer than
normal human fingers.

He still carries the Nordsee,
the iceland that it was,
in his nose:
everything remains in place,
as though it is
a plastic version
and has no interior.

He knows a world passes him by,
invisible supplicant,
holding cups of the liquor of itself
(fermented seaweed,
mown grass,
rosewater,
crude oil)
up to the oblivious hood of his nose.
And he loves the shapes of things,
what the mamaliga,
the dyed egg,
the plum brandy implies.

WATERBEACH

'...from Hermannstadt',
my grandma said, as
we passed their screen
of trees off the Ely road.
Up there, Cromwell's
house and the fens'
skeletal ship, the gaunt
cathedral, tilting glacially
into its anchorage like
Endurance. The road
a timeline, heading
back towards the civil
war, the devil springing
out of the bog,
Etheldreda. The garden

came into view. So did
they, Mrs Botradi stooped
between their beehives,
Mr Botradi in a plastic
chair, staring upwards
through circular shades,
a pair of black holes.
They stopped to take
each other in.
'Renate...'
Points of colour
on long stalks
wavering, concussed.
A street in Hermannstadt.
Honey. Cataracts.

THE LOTOS-EATERS

This was
after the war,
           or the war
had barely finished,

the sound of weapons
was still dying away;
           we came upon the neglected orchard,
overgrown but thriving, in the old compound of the farm.

This is what it means to abide, said the sage,
Bob of the Civil Service, falling to his knees
           in the last ash of the global cloud.
In that moment, when everything organised

stood in ruins, they were still scrumping fruit
in the unkempt plot, a pioneering association
           built out of the ashes of the war,
when the orchard stood in a good foot of the softest ash.

We came across them under the ash settling as if it were snowing.
I loved Bob. There, suddenly, was the redness of his heart;
           my grandparents, Renate, Nick, Joyce, Grandpa Chad,
all gathered around the table, presenting their shining apples

to Bob. The gun was smoking in the silhouette's hand
behind the blizzard, the first of the labouring shadows
           for whom we had fallen,
our eyes full of apples. You shot Bob. He joins my forebears.

Hello, said Henry, the features developing on his face,
this is my wife, Elizabeth, and looking into his eyes,
        looking into Elizabeth's sad eyes,
I did not want to get into the back of their van

or drive through the subtopian streets to their bungalow.
Elizabeth looked thrilled, or suppressed, with ash
        still on her wrist from the orchard.
Soon enough, we sat in their utterly foreign front room.

This is Mercer's Waterloo journal, said Henry, flicking through
a sheaf of brown sheets. But why did you have to kill Bob? I asked.
        To make another memory,
said Henry, brandishing a real Luger. This gun is German but

it lives in my hand. A pilot's leather hat came next,
then Baron von Richthofen's red leather shoes. Ducker & Sons,
        Henry said. The best shoes in the world.
Leaving, Richthofen brushed shoulders with Evelyn Waugh,

Evelyn Waugh in yellow shoes by Ducker & Sons, deep in the ledger,
stepping towards the Brideshead culmination, the private house
        pickled in common longing.
Henry disappeared behind a looted Iraqi banner depicting Saddam Hussein.

Revolutionaries come to this country, he said. It may have been hundreds
of years ago, it may as well be yesterday for all I care,
        and soon they get obsessed with mere reform.
I know a tonne of subversive people and they're terrific people,

they get to love how the laws are covered with moss, they love
how men educated together look longingly into one another's eyes
        and silently tell secrets about the constitution,
the glow of ginger in the smallest pot in a kitchen in Rustington.

Elizabeth fetched the banana, the clementine and the bar of dark
chocolate and secretly laid them on the mantelpiece in the hall,
          dwelling on the Canadians with roots in Worthing
and all along the south coast. I thought: they will murder me, too,

and this will be the truth of this quiet cul-de-sac, behind
the memorial to the man from Ford killed in an air accident outside,
          behind the damage done to events
by the passage of time. We have great, great people to remind us

about prioritisation in storytelling: Kemi, Michael, Niall, Liz;
we have the tales told by The National Trust to explain its purchases.
          Henry insisted I touch his panel of buckled metal;
there is no plot. I am not ready to stop now, I am not

ready to get off the train. In fact, I am only just getting started.
The best events in the imagination were all sorted like sweets
          by Thomas Malory
and they never, ever happened. Fuck you for making me scared,

Henry and Elizabeth. This is my revenge. I've no idea
if Renate felt fear, Jewish, cowering in Romania;
          if that is what her best friend felt,
scooping the last cabbage from the pot into her wet mouth and reducing

the Latin teacher to tears in the insoluble Bucharest apartment.
I still have the pot and sometimes a carbonised map of the lost world
          appears on its base when the latest soup has burnt;
there are Grandpa Chad and Joyce, released by love surprisingly late in life.

Nick, reading a map in the plane, saw a shadow move through the waters
and shook to think of the whiskey the living can taste in the bars of the carriers
          so released the museum's prize torpedoes
but it was only a whale and boy did it blubber when it blew up.

MISSING

Think about it, Jason said.
Memories have no depth.
Neither yours nor those
you learn to cherish.
They only yield themselves.
They are like names
on a memorial.
What's the substance?
A mass beneath,
general stone:
nothing that relates
to that specific name.

He told me then
about an exercise
he made his students do
at Thiépval, years ago –
to find their own name
somewhere on the stone
among the seventy-two
thousand other names.
That was when they stopped
dicking around and
reality came home.
No-one survived.

HEADSTONES

My phone lights up. A Malaysian number. Mina. I tilt downwards over the well again. Mells, obviously. Catkins hazing April, Somerset from branches parting. Suddenly past Lutyens, street view retrospect. Side-struck with morning sun, thudding through wild garlic in the valley, footholds of old sockets in stone. Close to wet stone, the smell of moss, of earth still moist in shade. Volume of breath. I spin round in the clearing and am struck again, concussed by a passing cloud. A Sopwith Camel over Cadbury Camp. The drifty hummocks they say were Camelot. The melting parallellogram of the Quantocks where we broke down.

*

Fragrances like melodies, orange lanterns leaching from my temples, the street trembling. Once, a letter would have taken four months to travel from London to Penang. Faster by opium clipper. A bottleneck of shipping lanes dotted through the Straits of Malacca, becoming a black glut. MALAY STATES in a banner across the landmass. Straits Settlements in small script in the sea. Mina in the George Town Festival office. Smoking a clove cigarette in the evening shade. Watching emails arrive in her inbox. Pressing delete. I shut my eyes and stand next to her for a second on that first night, in her hands. Blissfully passive.

*

One day we drove directly south, bypassing Shaftesbury, Blandford Forum, Bere Regis, and shot the arrow of our bounden sight right through the stately arch of Durdle Door. The breeze blew over frozen Tyneham. Coffee dripped in an earthernware pot. Mina walked back to the car, walnuts falling near the house, peaches closing over the claws of the boughs. At Montacute, Dicken looked up from the till, his eyes an explosion of irises. Agnosia of the beds. No forms but fading blues, yellows, creams, apricots, pinks, mauves, reds. White and obscure lenses hurrying up. The slow expansion of the reds. All flower and faceless.

*

Jason is off to the Front. Will I go with him? I remember that school trip so well, press-ganged by the luminous white graves. Then broken up and rearranged like earth, like cloud. German remains shovelled into a pit at Langemark. A grief not given room. A grief for which power could not stake out the relief of space. My teacher an absurd and statuesque ghoul among the accusatory oaks, the thousands of names. And it was the whites in the sky overhead that didn't move. The squat blocks in the ground began to drift. What were they teaching? Of course I'll go. Rolling round Picardy in a Mini listening to Lloyd Cole sounds like heaven.

*

MacDonald Gill at Pitzhanger Manor. A room full of low chatter like a sky full of Sopwith Camels. The Empire Marketing Board's first poster, Highways of Empire. MALAY STATES in a banner across the landmass. Straits Settlements in small script in the sea. Mina, lighting up. Then, distinct and bright white in the centre of the gallery, a War Graves Commission headstone. Gill's crisp lettering. A SOLDIER OF THE GREAT WAR KNOWN UNTO GOD. How many rows of those calling from Flanders and the Somme? Their glowing, solitary counterparts shining like mushrooms in English graveyards.

*

The majority are Portland stone but some are Hopton Wood limestone from Derbyshire, where they quarried to meet excess demand. Near Middleton, there are remnants of broken headstones in the walls. I stepped across my dreams up to the pile of concrete. White chips in miniature drifts. Needles in piles. Jason called back to say turn left at the end of the lane there, descend soundlessly into a sudden fir plantation, fall asleep in the front seats in April, May, June. Some month from the freshness of the year. I looked up from the jump leads to find myself flying over Tyne Cot with a pouch full of milk teeth for the boys.

*

The truth is not a headstone but a pit. Blank earth in the hollows of the body. Uncle Roy, escaping from a sinking submarine off Bastia, dying of his dreams in Rome. Hidden in the soil are small and loving models, holy sites plundered by soldiers in bright colours, the purples and yellows of spring, the postures of infancy crystallised as toys. What is remembered is what is forgotten, splitting from itself, turning in a different direction in the valley. I thought it was white as snow but it was red as blood, hundreds of white teeth turning in the eye of a red flower, whiteness misting to an uncountable array of red flowers.

*

The glacial segments of the fillets bristled as Jason unwrapped them from the waxed paper. Red and yellow light of nighttime. Mina and I walking like ghosts over frozen furrows in Blenheim Park hours before, steam billowing. Strange how I see it. Staring in from December darkness, breath wreathing my head. Me and Jason, marinaded in yellow light, talking by the sink. Fenugreek, cumin, fennel seeds spitting in a dented pan. The window frame buckling and curving, becoming circular. The ground loosening, tilting, becoming water. The house lurching, distending, becoming a clipper bound for Canton with its cargo of opium.

*

It is only in my memory that I feel so alone. In reality, Mina was waiting at the airport, standing with me in the queue for food. Time flowed over the weir. A row of cypresses against a red wall, its roots in our veins. Nepenthe. Helen relieving Telemachus and Menelaus of all memory of the war. Lin Zexu and Joseph of Arimathea holding hands on Glastonbury Tor, the drug pouring into the sea. All the solace in Benares, Patna, Malwa, burning in a meadow of trenches. Daoguang waking up to rumours of pests in metal ships from the West Ocean. Foxed by the size of his own empire. Where, in fact, was England?

*

Our stomachs were the lure of blankness. Ice and condensed milk browning with Malacca sugar. Pits of green noodles. A wound in slow motion walking through Bristol, Dover, Liverpool to the water. Up Mincing Lane and Exchange Alley. Sniffing at the threshold of Garraway's Coffee House. Drifting over remote earthworks, the infinite promise of a moment in time, the sky when you are high on a hill, infested with Sopwith Camels. Textile mills in the Midlands collapsing, slave ships repurposed as opium boats, the familiarity of the witch vanishing over the low wall on her broomstick, rounding the headland in an eggshell.

*

The row of cypresses, the red wall. There was an old love. The same love, in fact. A seam under the veil of the soil. But is there a brother to mourn in that specific grave? Uncle Roy, waking up from a sinking submarine to find himself falling from a window, already wrapped in his funeral shroud. Warmth weakens from the bedsheets like a fragrance. The row of cypresses. The red wall. I am clawing the ground, unable to explain the objects turning up in my hands. Underneath is one growing mouth, one building scream. But the noise is aborted, compressed into these teeth, these plastic toys, these flowers.

*

A whale vertebra from Zoology. A dip circle from the Whipple. A page of Southern Beech specimens from the Botanical Gardens. Rubbish rattling around among roots. I walked to the train station and the jungle went changelessly to ruins. Fussell's factory in Mells. Mina laughing through coins and portals of light. Jason rounding the corner in his Mini. Provisions spilt onto a checked cloth, demolished on a green in East Coker. I'd barely swallowed but I opened up again. Not the talking. Fish heads threw off their sauce and got up to levitate out. Oysters sped from omelettes. Coffees punched holes downwards out of time.

*

There are no headstones for what is under the ground, only for what is held at the surface. The place where my foot meets the gravel, where the plane hits the runway, where the sun touches the water. I will not call them by their names, their names cannot reach them. The whiteness of their faces mists into a red field. I am under the earth. This cemetery in which I stand at dusk, the sunset I drive off in: complications in the soil. Root, bone, scrap chandeliers. There are no headstones for what is under the name. A name, like a photograph, proof that memory fails. Roy, for example. Mina. There, that will do.

*

The night will be cool, hardening into winter. I'll stumble over a prone lad and go off, chilled. The ferry will be quiet, the light yellow. We'll be in Ypres on November 11 for the last post, eating eels full of spine out of a horribly thick cream sauce in the square. The first night we'll sleep near Albert, in the heart of the Somme. The second we'll spend in Poperinge, gateway to the battlefields of the Ypres Salient, billet for British troops. After dinner, I'll suddenly stand up, needing to breathe. I'll walk out into the square, take out my phone and dial a number. The bell will start ringing. Without warning, the square will flood.

*

Thousands of poppies appear and blossom into bulbs of smoke. Each bulb soon falls out of shape, rising, distending, blowing off. Through the haze, it becomes clear that there are also thousands of figures lying there beneath, blissed out beyond recollection, complete as stones. Understated bulbs of smoke flower from their mouths, carrying care, rephrasing memories as wordless dreams. Unthinkable objects. A smoke that freezes briefly in the reds of poppies, drifting up in thousands of trails like the aftermath of a bombardment. Others in the sky, drifting in giant shade like blimps, discover teeth, plastic toys, flowers.

*

The exhibition opened this evening. *Discovery*'s bell rang in celebration. I thought about Mina, what she was doing. I mean, she would have been asleep. But now. Early hours here. She'll have woken. She'll be walking through the streets before the heat, past the heritage pinks, blues, yellows of the shophouses. Picking up breakfast, shading her face. I walked home slowly after the guests had left, out beneath the MacDonald Gill domes. Lensfield Avenue deserted. On Parker's Piece, the lime trees trembled. In Reality Checkpoint's lemony glow, an enamoured soul sucked on their lover's neck. Flecks of scarlet on ice-white.

ALBERT

It's the clock tower I remember,
a thin and elegant clock tower
rising above a market square.

In January 1915,
a shell hit the spire
of the Basilica Notre-Dame de Brebières

in Albert.
It knocked the pinnacle's golden statue of the Virgin over
sideways, almost like an outstretched Mauser, Lee-Enfield or Berthier

but much bigger, and golder,
and a mother.
She stayed there,

offering her son to the soldiers,
until April 1918
when the whole church came a cropper.

After the war,
they rebuilt the structure
exactly as before.

It's not a clock tower
I remember
but that spire. The replica.

*

Jason and I sat in the dining room of a hotel in Albert
eating steak tartare
and talking about careers.

I wondered about becoming a government speechwriter.
Jason choked on his beer.
That's a hateful idea.

Why would you want to be one of those liars?
I saw his point and felt like a traitor,
thinking of how this room, now packed with diners,

must have been a great headquarters
for some villainous Gestapo brass, some minor Vichy mayor,
so plush and red like the set of a blockbuster.

Later, I realised – or remembered, rather –
with no surprise to speak of, just a tremor,
that, although Albert

was obliterated in the First World War,
immortalised by its tenacious Virgin, even mentioned by Borges, the writer,
it played no significant part whatsoever

in the Second. My favourite character
in *Saving Private Ryan* (Private Jackson, played by Barry Pepper)
is the sniper.

UP THE LINE

On our way to Bailleulmont,
we stopped in – I forget
the name. Some village.
Sunlight fell in two
squares on the bare
counter where

the barman put
the coffees, steam
opening in the
beams, mid-air.
I cleared my

*

throat. No
one left and
no one
 came

on the bare
platform. What
I saw

was Adlestrop –
only the

name.

BAILLEULMONT

There was an elderly man
directing the limp flow from a hose
at a headstone,
cleaning out lichen from the inscription.

Deserters – SHOT AT DAWN.
That's what it says
on their headstones.
But here is Albert.

10495 PRIVATE
INGHAM
MANCHESTER REGIMENT
1ST DECEMBER 1916

SHOT AT DAWN
ONE OF THE FIRST TO ENLIST
A WORTHY SON
OF HIS FATHER

The father turned off his hose
and told us with his arms
about bombs falling on this village in the forties
when he was a son.

INHERITANCE

Odours are how
interiors make themselves
known to the world.
My father lost his sense of smell
when, or was it because –
I know none of this firsthand.
I have pieced together what I can
from moments when clues
have offered themselves
discreetly. There –
the smell of fresh laundry.
In this way, I discovered how
my grandfather died,
failing to fix a simple problem
with the radio,
saying – he had not seen the figure
by the window – I'm an idiot.
The words rose quietly heavenward,
a speech scroll, and he fell towards
the surface of the earth, dead to
the passing pageant of fragrances
from his childhood in another country.

Every Easter,
my father takes eggs,
ties string around their shells
and boils them with onion skins
so that the boiled egg emerges
dyed, dressed in wild red
and pale crucifixes.
You take one,

I take the other.
I smash your egg with the nose of mine
and its crown crumples,
releasing the scent.
I had said something.
The Easter Acclamation
in a distant language.
Truly, he is risen,
is the reply. An echo through
a verandah in the hills
above Sibiu. In truth,
he was never dead.

FAMILY TREE

In Vlad Dracul's
veins – from whom
great uncle George
claimed our descent –
my blood beat
heavily. Outside,
a new forest
of Ottomans.
I woke. That
weight. Overnight,
on my breastbone,
some force had
made camp. Now,
they were impaled
in the past. I
harboured but
the dullest under-
song – like a weak
pulse – of bloodlust.

*

In New York,
I was the eyeballs
of my great uncle
George, selecting
books to spread
free market seed
in the USSR.
The best the West
could offer. How to fit

freedom in a suitcase?
Smuggle, compel it?
That was his problem
but bombs falling
on the Bucharest
he had owned,
in which my grand-
mother had hid,
were what reflected
in the shine of his eyes.
Je sème à tout vent.

*

In my chest,
Theresienstadt,
small light
from a window,
my great grand-
parents put
themselves
out.

*

In the shop
window, having
Renate's
eyes, I gazed
at the plenty
I couldn't afford,
stuffing my reflection.
Tomorrow, the boat
from Zeebrugge

to Hull. In my pocket,
the letter from me,
a 'maid',
to my best friend,
a 'lady'.
In my mouth,
my heart.

*

In Hull – his two boys,
Nick and George,
as yet but glints
in his dark, sad eyes –
Robert Minden
wondered which
side he was on,
Central or Entente.
The sun rose
so he ran.

*

In Farnham,
deathly pale,
my lady dismissed her
butler, remembering
her friend, her temporary
maid. Renate met Nick
in my front room.
George was suicidal
at the time.
Not yet working
for the CIA.

*

In the front
room at the wake,
the well-known
academic smiled
down. Paul loved
secular Jews but
kept them apart.
Don't you recognise
your dad? I did
and didn't, and bled.
There was his head,
making small talk,
so sure of the safety
of its perfect social
mask.

*

In the bungalow
on the remote
island, like a heart-
beat in a sea, I
step into
the room,
my mother
and father.
Because dreaming
of what was is
also passionate,
at dawn
the vampires
leave.

MICRO

I get home from school and speak
to Bella. This dreadful Sherlock Holmes
story, I say. Holmes,
she says. That makes me think of
Carlo Ginzburg, the Italian historian.
Carlo Ginzburg says of history
that concreteness is both its strength
and limit. Later,
I'll read on:
it can't employ the powerful
and terrible tool of abstraction.
Narrative emerged from tracks, he says,
footprints in the mud made into clues
by hunters marking traces
for the story of each
flight. So he points to Sherlock Holmes,
to Helen Stoner turning up at Baker Street,
legible.
The spatter-pattern on her skirt.
She left at six,
reached Leatherhead at twenty past
and came in by the first train to Waterloo.
Pray go on with your narrative,
says Holmes to Stoner, her eyes
like those of some hunted animal.
The glazed eyes of my class,
poor kids, putting up with this
shit. You see it, Watson? The speckled
band! A swamp
adder. The deadliest snake in India.
Sir William Herschel, employing fingerprints
as signatures. Concrete, yet

abstracting. From Bengal to the Transvaal,
England pulsing in the shadows with its
records. Later, I'll sit down
with dinner. Agatha Christie's Poirot
runs the title,
her signature slanting forward.
Graphologists confer. The hands of Hyde
and Jekyll. Extroversion.
Do you need eggs to make gnocchi?
I ask Bella, hunting for a recipe.
In this way, concrete concerns
displace abstraction. Just potatoes
in water. Yes, school is tough, refracted through
the ruins of November, the class restive,
Lewis stomping in like a hammer,
birdshit down his back,
Harry rounding off the sketch of his
detective, laughter moving from one face
to another like a fingerprint until
whose face is whose? Red shift.
Poirot phase.
Though Holmes is passable,
Harry prefers the Belgian sleuth,
rounding off his story with –
that's when they found him
on the kitchen floor. The dead
chef; Poirot
drying off the egg cup with morose
precision unaware he had dislodged the toxin
hidden in the vessel. Harry –
punctuation. Re-
read. Slit elf, from Amun-Ra.
Harry Quest. Hear that?
Sasquatch. That's

the curse-whoosh from the tomb-cave.
Did for the whole expedition and they put –
put concrete over the cave-mouth
(wherein darkness abstracts)
petulantly. Still, Poirot
polishes, cycling through
the marked corpses of his repertoire
as they arch like rigor-bridges over
nothing,
bloated, poisoned,
shot in the head. Barely audible –
echoes of other, similar histories.
The plot thickens. The Speckled Band
gets its fingerprints all over
class. I fret.
Bella – this story, it's monstrous.
A woman, murdered for mystery.
A native butler, murdered for backstory.
A whole caravan of red herrings read
out of the tea leaves,
out of what the tea leaves leave
behind: stains. When Poirot finally does bend down,
just skirting indignity,
to peel the flesh-like mask from the face of the imposter,
the so-called dead chef – well done,
Harry, achievement point –
who should it be under that flim-flammery,
that rubbery scam frontispiece,
that Hammer horror façade forehead, but –
gosh it –
Sherlock Holmes himself, his face
his fingerprint. Alive.
And what should we make of the fallen?
Why are they dead?

ITS MOUTH WORKING

The thought that
a dog-leg
of the front line
ran through here;
the thought that
men died
all over the place,
in dreadful ways,
in the space
across which
we now sit;
the thought that
this was a site
of carnage:
that thought
makes me
feel good,
said our host,
tearing up.
This is a weird
bed and breakfast,
I thought,
setting my
gin and tonic
on the sideboard.

*

The walls were lined
with books about the war,
biographies of bigwigs,

works on military strategy,
accounts of landmark battles.
We came here to be closer
to this energy, said our
other host, silhouetted,
leaning in from the window seat.
Can you feel it?
There were fields outside,
the wind moving
in them like a shoal.
We came here to be closer
to the echoes. Echo.
Not memory.
The word that returns.
Can you hear it?
Jason swapped his legs over,
crossing his right with
his left. I never feel
comfortable in
that position, I thought.
Not very far away at all:
the mute crater.

BETA ELEMENT

Nothing is as lusty
as the singing
of an English beard.

Never has an apple
dripped so much.

OPIOID

I woke up this morning,
my throat was a bit tight
and I wondered if I had another cold.
But I had a cup of tea and a piece of fruit
and blew my nose and it was fine.
So passed Church Stretton and Craven Arms,
Ludlow, Leominster and Hereford
      and this was not something I thought about long
and the city of mist,
unvanquished by morning,
did not remember them.

Near Abergavenny, a town owes
its interiors to one man,
a carpenter. This white room
in the garden has no ceiling,
nothing to defend the piano
from the poppies that drift
in their hundreds out of the sky.
      What has gone into the past has gone
into the mist and recurs
like he does, on his slow walk to the noose,
smoke rising from his shin.

It is special when you go over the top
and you start to go down
and suddenly you see the sea.
Going down to the sea at the boring
familiar ports is what is depressing
but there are all sorts of parts of the coast
where this grey beginning happens sedately,

      when the land forgets about itself
and what extends to the horizon
is a landscape
you can still people.

I came to the boardwalk, to the reserve
of vegetated shingle, and the glass rooms
of the shoreside houses were largely empty
but some contained statues.
That is why I lay for weeks
hardly moving in the healing room
watching the shadow of the tree translate
      wind into light on the white wall, flowers
drifting down into the summerhouse
covering the piano, the rigid Edwardian chair,
my Edwardian headwound

which opened as a memorial in 1920.
It was used as a community cottage,
a hospital serving poppies
in the form of holy smoke,
in the form of strong, forgetful tea,
in the form of fentanyl,
confused by synthetic longing
      for a home it never came from.
I can play one of Schubert's impromptus badly;
I can speak French badly;
I can read Italian badly;

I even have a feeling for German.
Is there anybody there, said the traveller?
I sit at the keyboard depressing,
too softly for sounds,
the keys in my mouth.

I walk around Cardiff and I own the place:
    an excellent place for my knights to dance.
With the success of his tea shop,
my father has provided me with so much.
I should be grateful but I am not.

PRIVATE SKY

Rain spreads across
the canopy as trees
close over the path
that village made of
cloud, the secrecy
of close high trees,
thin stems of their
memorial, the list
of their private
green, the manor
disappearing behind
its walls, our dreams
spreading out over
the rise, a squad
mown down by rain.

AFTER-GLOW

after Ivor Gurney

Reaching Langemark cemetery,
we stood in the shade of an oak
to eavesdrop on a muscular man
instructing six cadets, in English,
in how to enfilade. This is how
you enfilade. He crossed his forearms,
held them out. I couldn't read it

      passed into the dusk
Time passed from mind
      Time died
from Framilode, fremd
      fremde Zeit
the cooler hush after the strafe
      Severn and Somme

but the six boys swivelled their
heads. A small wind moved in
the trees (all grief-stricken, German
oaks) and over the flat, grey
graves. The length of the Friedhof.
This is how you enfilade
the field of pre-dead agreed.

GURNEY DRIVE, PENANG

There was an outdoor gym
near the pier. We went there.
Did we have an argument?
I can't remember why
we went. Were we speaking?
I can't hear anything. All there is
is the gym gear and us
standing there, present but
absent. Two reeds from
the opium-dependent fens.
A hallucination from
Grasmere. I saw sailors
moving around as though
it were a film set. It was
a film set. I put on my frock coat
and turned to go. The ship
was sailing shortly.
                UNESCO
hovered in the present like a sunset,
over the future like a UFO.

NEMESIS

The iron steamer *Nemesis*, built in Liverpool for the Secret Committee of the East India Company and launched on the Mersey in 1839, enabled the British to butcher the Chinese almost effortlessly. As well as being full of guns and made of metal, its shallow draught allowed it further upstream in the silty waterways around Canton than could have been anticipated. This enabled it to add the element of surprise, and the psychological impact of shock, terror and demoralisation, to its literal firepower.

The Chinese called it the devil ship.

*

The Chinese had no navy to speak of. Their war junks were unsteady, old and unable to venture out onto deep waters. In the words of an Englishman, they were

> large, unwieldy looking masses of timber – painted red and black, with large goggle eyes in the bows – useless, save in smoothest water –

> To convey to the mind of a stranger the ridiculous excess of the inutility of the naval establishment of China would –

> be impossible.

*

A record of the exploits of the *Nemesis* was made by an Englishman. En route to the front line the *Nemesis* stopped, like other boats heading to or from Canton for trade or war, at the island of Penang.

> Penang is very properly considered one of the loveliest spots in the eastern world, considering its limited extent; and, from the abundance and excellence of its spice productions, which come to greater perfection in the straits than in any other part in which they have been tried (except, perhaps, in the island of Java), this little island has proved to be an extremely valuable possession. It abounds in picturesque scenery, heightened by the lovely views of the opposite coast of Malacca, called Province Wellesley, which also belongs to the East India Company.

*

, the governor drowned in a small pool,

, half-smoked pipes, cups of untasted tea, abandoned pots of tea,

, throwing monkeys with dynamite off ships,

, sky of green stars,

, old and honeycombed guns,

, last one out, shoot the captain in the head,

*

, whoever is wounded or falls in battle

becomes a demon in a foreign land,

RE-ENACTMENT

As I remember, I was a woman
and you were a man. I had come to say
farewell. I was to leave without delay.
What future did we have? You were the man;
the smokers, Chinese; the drug, Indian.
My home was very, very far away.
I hoped, perhaps, we'd meet again one day.
You looked at me like a historian.

The escalator led out of the past
and into the future. I watched you shrink
as I went down towards security.
Were you crying? Anyway, the jet blast
knocked me back into my seat from the brink
of fancy. Back towards futurity.

*

As I remember, I was Boudica
and you were the Roman Empire. The flame
of my outrage burnt fiercely. Yours, the blame.
I shut my eyes in Little India
to see mist in blue-green East Anglia
rise, the fervour of rebellion claim
London, the legion slaughter us all. Shame
I had to remember I was not her

and could not die in a brilliant display
of oppositional failure. As we stood,
I knocked my cup. Cold tea made a lake.
A sea. I knew Boudica's future history.
My briefly complicated fury would
abbreviate to something pure and fake.

*

As I remember, I was King Arthur
and you were Avalon, the apple-blessed,
the island I would go to for my rest.
I don't mean you. I mean the *idea*
of you. You yourself were getting smaller
on the shore I left behind, heading west,
with my grievous head wound and a heaving chest.
The traffic passed on Lebuh Chulia;

the sun set. I slept until my nation
bid me wake: the stewardess said we're here,
gently shaking me. I left the cabin,
crossed the border and sat at the station,
recalling my last words to Bedivere:
for in me is no trust for to trust in.

*

As I remember, I was King Alfred,
cake-failer. All you had asked me to do
was keep them from burning. They were burnt through.
Your accusation could not be refuted
so all I did was mutely bow my head,
forcing the work of anger onto you.
This sovereign strategy was not new:
it was something I had inherited

from my dad. Privately, I blamed
the vikings for having distracted me
with their Great Heathen Army. The waiter
brought round more dim sum. You were done. Ashamed,
I reassured you. Wessex *would* be free.
I knew. I felt a native greatness stir.

*

As I remember, I was King Harold.
My place in history was loss. Defeat.
I had lost sight of you. The arrow-sleet
had lodged a blighter in my eye and bowled
me roundly over. I was going cold,
conked among ankles, the wash of retreat,
the piles of housecarls and the horses' feet.
I felt middle-aged. I would not grow old.

There you were. Three stalls further on, unphased
by the downpour, browsing the piles of dry
fish. Arrowheads with eyes. Ikan bilis.
They shot me a volley of glares. You raised
your head. I was fine: grit in the eye. (A lie.)
How would I see myself through this?

*

As I remember, you were a woman.
I was a man who wished to philander -
nay, had done so. Out on the veranda,
I clutched at your severe hands, at your fan,
and at your slender gloves, like Peter Pan
with all of my milk teeth shining and a
headline in my heart, the propaganda:
boys will be boys; a man must be a man.

Suddenly, I remembered where I was.
But what had become of my future spouse
and the empire line of her cotton gown?
I was not in England. I knew because
I'd lost sight of the facade of the house,
the landscape by Capability Brown.

*

As I remember, I was Robin Hood
bewitched by a leg of tandoori chicken.
You laughed, well-travelled. Sherwood's mutton
was a world away. This was real food.
But who *were* you, hooded and strange? You stood.
Good God, my heart. Richard! Coeur de Lion,
returned to undo John's bad law, to champion
the native disobedience of good.

We loved each other. The love was strong.
In the home wood, I controlled my arrows;
you went abroad with the cross. Violence
clears the ground for good and bad, right and wrong.
Devils, we knew that when it comes to blows
the first blow is always made *in defense*.

As I remember, you were King Henry
the Fifth and I was Prince Hal, the younger
you. I lay late in bed. You got up before
the day grew hot. I joined you, eating roti
at a roadside table. I was hungry.
You were full. We stared past each other,
the empty space between us like a mirror
and a time machine. You knew me

not. You were full. I was hollow.
The chef span dough out expertly behind
your head. A crown. For me, just bread and sack.
My roti came. I chewed but couldn't swallow
without grimacing. Facing, our outlines aligned.
But you'd grown up. And I was at your back.

As I remember, I wept as your head
came off, rubbing the tears into my face.
O Essex, you paragon of disgrace.
Too long deferred, our hopes had died. You dead,
they lived again, pale-faced, inverted,
forever virtual. As such, solace
of the hurting kind. I couldn't displace
your face as I undressed and went to bed.

Sir Francis Drake stepped off the Golden Hind
with a cigarette and a pomme de terre,
saying these are for you, my Virgin Queen;
the worst is still ahead, the best behind,
now faith is the ground of things which are hoped for,
and the evidence of things which are not seen.

*

As I remember, my head was right round.
You were the monarchy, come to a head:
you had to be decapitated
and your false investiture rewound.
This achieved, I would find myself unbound
by mastering love. The plane descended:
England. I could not see the hatred
on which my love was built; which my love crowned.

I pressed my face to the window, a male
gazing through a national spectacle.
A thousand miniature buildings. Back here,
I would agonise over my new model
with the mania of a just radical,
neither leveller nor cavalier.

*

As I remember, we were both women
and, talking, we took a turn around the
room, and then another and another,
until the horrid walls began to spin,
and the tedious pianist, an in-
law, disappeared into the wallpaper
with the tea set, the jam from Oxfordshire
and the final, unappealing muffin.

We sat down on the hillside. I reclined
in your lap in order to look up at
your perfect face. But I couldn't see much.
Just a blur. Affection had made me blind.
Only your voice steadied my breathing. That,
and that warmth on my cheek, my chest. Your touch.

*

As I remember, I was Lord Nelson.
Leaving was a battle I'd win but die
winning, thereby coming to underlie
my win. Dying: a myth's best foundation.
Nothing better than a corpse to build on,
not even a tip-top career. Goodbye.
I turned away, descending peremptorily
into the cask in which the concoction

that would preserve my body sloshed. Brandy,
camphor, myrrh. Before me swam departure.
Doha. London. Duty-free. I cracked a smile,
thinking of the duty I had done my country
and the time I bowled a yorker with a
cannonball at the Battle of the Nile.

*

As I remember, I was Wellington.
Did it surprise you? Here we were again,
parting. I could hardly hide my disdain.
Good luck in the South Atlantic Ocean
I thought, turning back to European
civilization, the map on the plane,
my face reflected in the screen. The strain
told behind my statuesque expression,

one eye on Brussels; my chin over Spain;
the wide world, off-screen. Poor Napoleon,
never again to see France. I winced. A pain
in my temple. So much for the Panthéon,
imperial pretension, that Charlemagne
shit. My throat hurt. It was the air condition.

*

As I remember, we were not amused.
Where was our bag? The carousel ran on.
We hadn't time. We had to get to Osborne
House. Bleary in the white light, we confused
the furthest carousel with the pier we used
at Gosport. A little, waiting boat. The setting sun.
Ryde beginning to twinkle on the horizon
as the coastline and the Solent fused

into nighttime. I blinked. I was alone
in Heathrow. Morning. There was no we
to speak of. No bag either, that was clear:
the only thing in baggage reclaim was the drone
of the carousels going round, empty.
Somewhere, the sun was setting. But not here.

*

As I remember, I was the Light Brigade.
I'd lost my charger under the bed.
I lay in the valley of death, phone dead,
between my unpacked bag and the frayed
edge of the hostel sheet. The streetlamp made
an image on the ceiling, orange-red.
A mouth. The mouth of hell. Good youth misled
into absurd assays. The rainfall of the cannonade.

You got back. In a flash, things came together.
I surveyed my scattered clothes, your ankles framed
in the doorway, the skirting clouded with damp.
Battery-smoke blew in tatters across Crimea.
Breath plumed in the ward. Suddenly there flamed,
like a siren, the light of your undaunted lamp.

*

As I remember, you and I were men.
You came striding down Lorong Love, the brass
buttons twinkling on your blue, naval dress.
We spent the night in an opium den.
Our dreams that night were a strange expansion.
We lay curled together on a tideless
shore, almost afraid of the stars, the stress
of uniform discarded. We kissed. Then,

the Thames disclosed itself in the dawn light;
neither was it the nineteenth century.
We were not lovers, though we had been lent
the memory. We were gentle, polite,
disabused. Longing has its history,
however complicit, in the present.

PAINKILLER

I never saw you as a soldier,
asleep in the long grass, the flower of your dream
   paused over your head like a cloud.
But I feel your chest exploding
   every time I hold you now.

   You cannot imagine the memory
I keep of our friendship, of lying on our backs
   in the summer grass in Grantchester,
our tongues the wicks of extinguished candles,
   the blue umbrella laid aside.

   Close by – perhaps a mile off –
my recollection gathers. Punt poles on the river
   mimic snapped masts and trajectories,
the trashing of Chinese junks. Kowloon. Chuenpi.
   Thoughts by England given.

   My smoke drifts over the water.
Floating warehouses off Lintin island and boats
   along the riverbank dispense crates
of sticky, brown shot for the bowls of the interior.
   The years, the centuries, blend and blur.

   I feel the cotton against my skin.
I turn on my side to you, your still civilian limbs.
   Snow White, suspended in your coffin.
A forest of thorns, a rooftop of roses, me
   and the penetrable walls.

From this remembered body,
I recall the future: you sign up for this,
    you consent to get shot first
(the old lie, dulce et opium est)
    to protect your country, others' pacifism,

    the nation of sombre jaws and brows
on Remembrance Sunday, the way the British dead
    stand for all war dead, honestly,
planted as clay poppies in the green moat of the Tower,
    remembrance an anaesthetic haze

    spreading like spilt tea across the map of the world.
The use to which a purchase is put does not concern the merchant.
    You buy a poppy, you respect that.
In a moment of silence, I look up from my desk to see
    a population transfixed before the clock face.

    A soldier now, you really could explode,
could murder for the tedium of my present life
    and the empire of its memories,
returning, sheathed in the unending fiction
    of relief, to Grantchester.

ROYAL ENGINEER

Starting uphill
    I lift my head to judge
the rise
    a gentle slope and striking elm
two white men in its shade
    the table laid
for tea and on the white cloth
    marmalade
a sunset flame
    and in the marmalade
inch-high
    a soldier caught
head over heels
    where have you been
our red-eyed son?
    I have been walking
fathers
    over Oxford
in the school inspector's dreams
    examining
the hedgerows
    tender burdock
trespass
    sometimes for the fire-black shades of God
to stare down at me
    pin me to the bridge
and some young
    piteous murdered face
to pass reflected on the glassy pond I cross
    to tread among the estuaries

the Thames
    the Medway
Chatham
    Rochester
where Bishop Gundulf
    first King's Engineer
looks on with blank and acid-eaten eyes
    in stone
the White Tower of his memory
    the Board of Ordnance
twinkling
    in his inch-wide eyes
the view
    from French
is ordered or ordained
    terrain that is surveyed
is owned
    the first rule of the conqueror
sweet William
    Bastard
William Rufus
    Henry Uno
chain of knowhow
    province of the engineers
the hill to Gillingham is sapper-swarming
    though I cannot touch
the bodies of their countless dead
    I walk into the Royal Engineers Museum
a row of Bosch heads looking shocked
    a line of targets
used to harden eyes against
    the human look
how long an inch-long
    bullet hole

I tread the galleries
       between
the sightless eyes exhibits are
       the plunder from
the Arrow War
       the Summer Palace
in Haidian
       Beijing
its knives
       and pipes
and inch-high deities
       including Vaishravana
god of wealth
       triumphal banner in his right hand
mongoose spitting jewels in his left
       no trace of violence but
the stuff itself
       the mute
a mile
       an inch
across the map
       the very catalogue that cultivates
an inch
       objects
all quiet at the V&A
       and in the same museum going
under
       Gundulf's sightless eyes
all white
       the Ordnance Survey
coming true
       the Highlands
under detail
       under order

Prestonpans but then
	Culloden
Lord Lovat
	off shovel
into mapless childhood
	mountains
men the mirror of the barren
	and impassable
the Ordnance Survey
	born exterminating Jacobites
we do not sleep
	in whole skins
Watson
	Roy
one inch
	a thousand yards
a stare
	the map
of the estate
	we know it now
you will not get it back
	my pipe is lost
but south from Manchester
	the Aranda
Gangalidda Garawa
	Nyamal
and Yawaru
	are returned
their sacred objects
	without reservation
suddenly
	the land slopes downwards and towards
the right
	how would the contours show it

somewhere
    it is hard to find
a decent map
    the sea
and reach the downs of Picardy
    where every Tory flashback starts
and fathers
    in their whites
become their blood
    God help us if we fail to pay our debt
in fullest full
    proceeds the doggerel
it's Beaumont-Hamel
    folks
a Fokker
    a Snipe
and a Bentley Camel
    mangled feet
walk all day long
    head bowed
and cut wire by the apple tree
    silhouettes
ran up to die
    some tempestuous morn in early
July
    one shoulder forward
in the different hail
    as though Newfoundland's
kindly blizzard
    not
a primal burst
    come with the volleying
no way
    not lolling high

from Hinksey to the hill
    but mud shot through
with a blossom of eyes
    and later Chinese Labour Corps recruits
collected up inches of bone
    and tatters of
the uniforms
    of rotted young
perhaps not there
    and died themselves
Noyelles-sur-Mer
    Shi Zaoji
these friends and colleagues
    incomparable
the corner of a field and
    summarised
for inspiration
    Captain Truelove studied
hard Chinese exhibits in
    British Museum
sightless eyes
    where do you really come from
never been
    the gravestones with their Chinese
characters
    their inch-long
do not understand
    I make these links because
they make themselves
    take up our quarrel
out of me
    you can't keep circling the point
false star
    you give an inch

they take a
    while
no point or if there is
    it's something
four dimensional in three
    those spaceships
Cixin Liu describes
    expiring in a foreign frame
or then again
    the prospect when
you step from three dimensions
    into four
translated by a Reddit user
    from the Mandarin
in the fragment
    of an inch
the depth has become
    limitless

PÉRONNE

Jason and I stood on a massive reproduction
of Europe in 1914. Jason was on Greece

looking across Austria-Hungary to Berlin.
I had just come in and was in the Bay of Biscay.

The map took up the whole floor, but cases on the walls
presented some contextual material culture.

A three-tiered diorama of soldiers annexing
Madagascar for the French in 1896.

A German lithograph of the English attacking
the Boers, featuring a notable barbed wire fence.

A Dutch board game, *Boer en Rooinekspel*, where you
moved counters around the beards of ugly soldiers' heads.

A diorama showing the Russo-Japanese War,
the first *modern* war, with lead soldiers tipped over, dead.

A shooting game patented by Emile Fritz, Paris,
in which you popped a cork bullet at national flags.

*

The rosettes, hats, beer jugs, ribbons and medals of all
the bright cadets, reservists and conscripts of Europe.

QUEBEC

Watching a drunk Brit
with *Lest We Forget*
stitched into the sleeve
of his polo shirt
stumble around and burble
at the Menin Gate
in Ypres
for the last post,
Jason said

*

I forget what he said.

THE OLD VICARAGE, GRANTCHESTER

Back home
I spent every morning
crying, returning to
the room in George
Town where we
slept, falling
asleep and waking
there, getting up, having
a shower, drying,
floating to the hawker
frying oysters, eating
in the open air with you
until I came to

in the square in England
I still sat in, crying as if
there were no
history, only summer
weather so sheer
the world was remade
in that causeless
image and absolutely
convinced of its
sufficiency,
forgetful of
the world it took
to dream itself.

THE REVEREND GREEN

You must remember, these songs were always old,
Sir Orfeo. Under the grene wode lynde, where
the thought-dead go, sardining themselves
three miles through a cave past Winchester.
Through the woodland shade, a green fin moves,
no face beneath, only an ancient corn dolly
riding a silver arrow in the reign of mystic Babylon,
King John, in Sherwood Forest and the paths
he knew, each one, every tree a pillar of song,
a cloud of leaves. But silence reigned,
all sounds long gone, not even one bird sang
and the ground was a uniform shade of green.

Near Sherwood, in silence, a cannonball clipped
the steeple of St Mary Magdalene. Another halved
Baron Dohna, standing on a barge in the Trent.
All along the Great North Road smoke rolled
from cannon mouths, circling Newark with a flower.
In the fields around, brewers kept waltzing.
I came to dressed as a Roundhead so kept concealed
my desire to spend the crown jewels on an army
and land at Bridlington despite it all, titling myself
melodiously Her She-Majesty, Generalissima,
and trying, trying without voice, to bombard the sky,
its many-headed lead and iron, with a pioneering aria.

Moving sinuously north towards a fork in the A1,
my best image of singing was the two slender
chimneys of Ferrybridge C emitting helplessly.
Moving punitively towards the Southern Hemisphere,
my best image of a chimney was Guy Pearce in *Priscilla*

trailing foil from his great stiletto as the bus rolled on.
Things are different now, or should be. I am an
entire person, an intersection of cheese wires
anchored in the present perimeter. But huge dolls
keep falling out of history and getting mandolined.
In the market square, the cobbles are shining
and the butcher speaks through a microphone

but the unravelling clouds make no noise.
The most confusing comfort: that death can take
the form of a beguiling retinue, a river curling
through its floodplain, a forest, frith with flours,
or the dead curls of a curtailed flow,
Cuckmere Meander, museum peace, the water
beginning to stare at the sky like an oil slick,
the permanent sense of something impending,
the songs of engines starting up. What grows
is terrifying and stealthy, asparagus tips farmed
by muscular salmon, dead-eyed concrete throats
throwing themselves up all over the atlas,

forced rhubarb, the whole roster of Elizabethans
suddenly floating free from their portraits, ruffs
rotating, drifting up into the clouds like a family
of self-decapitating progenitors. At some point,
smoke turns to hope, a pretext for more smoke,
a pollutant way of imagining transfiguration.
But before, during and after that, fragments
with baffled origins, unsung syllables, go tumbling
into the flames, and the chimneys look like trunks
and the smoke looks like bunches of green leaves
and the roots grow so slowly, whatever they are,
that the song they sing extends into silence.

BRIGHTON POPPIES

after Eileen Myles

Then a row of you
up against the wall.
This or
that, this
or that.
Some are red,
shaded, singing.
Others are colourless
and historical.
But all of them I
and they trail off
for their beautiful
statues.

*

21/08/20

Vahni – Time passes, and drops the keystone in the arch.

Bion – We looked at the maps again. They were exact and clear; the cursed place where we stood was not.

> Of this, at least, I feel assured, that there is no such thing as *forgetting* possible to the mind.

> To my architecture succeeded dreams of lakes – and silvery expanses of water.

> The sea appeared paved with innumerable faces.

Packing up the Rose Hill Terrace flat, found a box Mina made me for my 21st birthday. Brilliantly assembled. Ocean of blue tissue paper. Special places cut out from Ordnance Survey maps, stuck on the lid in the sea, a kind of imaginary island cluster: Mells, Cadbury Castle, Cadbury Camp, Stourhead. Parallelogram of the Quantocks. No Penang, though, obviously. Almost surprised.

Thinking about the trip w/ Jason shortly after that. Some of that countryside so like Sussex. Up the hill to Shoreham camp – write to him re/ that Yasmin Khan book before school starts. Kat and I about to head out to meet Ella and James. Lyme Regis tomorrow to see Ralph. Hollingdean from Monday.

Gogmagog   Gog and Magog   Gog from Magog
sheep paddock and memorial fringe
   AstraZeneca   field expanse
     62nd tallest tree in England
Saxon Road   Cellarer's Chequer
                 old store for the fat abbots
        skylarks nesting in long daisies
narwhal tusk through the brain of the crown cauliflower
                  sovereign community of
         chalk pit
          poppies
        anti-bark collar
  Cambridge Assessments   Massucco Buttress
    blossom in the reactionary orchard

CONDITIONAL

The day they tore down Colston, we were standing
on Marwick Head staring at the surface of the sea.
If we'd been there several days before,
we'd have seen a pod of killer whales passing.
If we'd been there a century ago, we'd have seen
Lord Kitchener's ship,
Hampshire,
strike a mine left by a U-boat
and sink with him on board.
Now, we stood by his memorial,
a castlelike tower,
watching thousands of birds fish.
You're burning, you said, handing me the sun cream.
You remind me of my dad, I replied.
His hairless, at-risk head,
array of hats. Let's head down for a swim.
A fishing boat, reverie-small.
If we'd been there a thousand years
ago, it would have been a Viking longship. Now,
Viking ruins huddled under mounds around the bays,
ruffled by the cyber-wind of supremacist fantasy
blowing as far as Vinland – North America
before Columbus, who was soon to fall in Richmond,
Baltimore, St Paul and lose his
head in Boston. If you can
keep your head –.
We started down towards the shore.
Over the headland, another site
stood scoured by the wind:
Skara Brae. If we'd been there in 1772,
Joseph Banks, *Endeavour*'s naturalist,

would have been digging it.
Now, starlings held it.
There were no visitors.
Hwaer cwom mearg? Hwaer cwom mago?
Hwaer cwom maþþumgyfa? Hoarder.
I thought vaguely backwards, Cecil Rhodes
about two hundred yards away,
my old teacher, hungover,
leaning over a page of Anglo
Saxon, the present, active snow
of Marwick Head, the seabird colony,
insistent as a substrate. I tried
to share a morbid reverie – If I should die –
but found this was an accidental Rupert Brooke
quote, so started again. If I die before you –
you reached across
to wipe traces of suncream off my nose –
scatter my ashes off this cliff.
You rolled your eyes.
A fulmar swung close on patrol.
You sound like your mum, you said –
talking of her ashes dissolving
in the waters off
Port Bàn – White Port – Iona,
round the coast from the White Strand of the Monks
where Vikings had massacred many holy men
in the tenth century,
blood pinking the sand.
Some want to burn, when dead. Others,
like my mother's parents, choose burial,

*

if they're free to choose. BRITONS
YOUR COUNTRY NEEDS YOU.
I looked back at Kitchener's turret.
The Battle of Jutland.
Early summer, 1916. If I should die
think only this of me. Or, calling from the other side
of grief – Have you news of my boy Jack?
Rudyard Kipling wrote the phrase cut
into the bleached headstones of the nameless dead.
A SOLDIER OF THE GREAT WAR
KNOWN UNTO GOD.
And, for the war memorials,
THEIR NAME LIVETH FOR EVERMORE –
Book of Ecclesiasticus.
So many men, so many sons,
down into the broken
surface of the earth, called to death
by Kitchener. I felt the closeness of the whiteness
of my skin to stone. Some imposition
hard to name. As though I was
already dead, googling Kipling's 'If',
tabs open on the constant tearing down
of Colston, rage sending flames into the police
logic of America. Above the doors to Central Court:
If you can meet with Triumph and Disaster –
those stooges dressed in suitable attire, entirely
white, a code owed to the apt Victor-
ians – And treat those two imposters just the same.
Stop looking at your phone, you said.
Reminded suddenly of what I was
missing, I stopped.
A neighbourhood of statues
I'd always thought
silent. Now I heard the silence for the whispering

it was. If after if. Not the first
conditional. The third. Soft
fall-down of inheritance. Hateful
baseline of parental love. Yours is the Earth
and everything that's in it.
If you'd been harbourside in Bristol
as the slave ships docked,
totting up the yearly income,
if you'd been of that place,
of that time,
why of course, my son –
this is how it was –.
We reached the beach and swam.
Our skin shone like seals-
kin. If you can force your head
under the water, foam like milk,
hold in the scream.

Words or phrases from the following texts are used in the poems.

The Pilgrim's Progress, John Bunyan • *Reflections on the Revolution in France*, Edmund Burke • 'A gramaphone on the subject', Denise Riley • A letter from Edwin Lutyens to his wife Emily Lytton • *Where Poppies Blow*, John Lewis Stempel • 'To Opium', Maria Logan • 'Poppies', Sara Coleridge • *Narrative of the Expedition to China*, John Elliot Bingham • *The Opium War Through Chinese Eyes*, Arthur Waley • 'The Dead', Rupert Brooke • *Wolf Solent*, John Cowper Powys • 'Highways of Empire', Empire Marketing Board poster designed by MacDonald Gill • Imperial War Graves Commission headstone designed by MacDonald Gill • *Hot Books in the Cold War: The CIA-Funded Secret Western Book Distribution Program Behind the Iron Curtain*, Alfred Reisch • 'Laventie', Ivor Gurney • *Severn and Somme*, Ivor Gurney • 'Adlestrop', Edward Thomas • Albert Ingham's headstone, Bailleulmont Communal Cemetery • 'Morelli, Freud and Sherlock Holmes: Clues and Scientific Method', Carlo Ginzburg • 'The Speckled Band', Sir Arthur Conan Doyle • *The House on the Hill*, Cesare Pavese • 'On Reading *Blake: Prophet Against Empire*', Geoffrey Hill • 'The Listeners', Walter de La Mare • *The Chinese Repository, Vol. 5* • *The Nemesis in China, Comprising a History of the Late War in the Country; with an Account of the Colony of Hong Kong*, William Dallas Bernard • *The Opium War*, Julia Lovell • *Works*, Sir Thomas Malory • Hebrews 11:1, The Geneva Bible • 'The Soldier', Rupert Brooke • 'The Old Vicarage, Grantchester', Rupert Brooke • 'The Cenotaph', Charlotte Mew • *Map of a Nation: A Biography of the Ordnance Survey*, Rachel Hewitt • 'Thyrsis: A

Monody, to Commemorate the Author's Friend, Arthur Hugh Clough', Matthew Arnold • Verses inscribed on a plaque at the entrance to the Beaumont-Hamel Newfoundland Memorial, John Oxenham • 'In Flanders Fields', John McCrae • *Death's End*, Cixin Liu • *Silencing the Past: Power and the Production of History*, Michel-Rolph Trouillot • *Learning from Experience*, Wilfred Bion • *Sir Orfeo* • 'New York Tulips', Eileen Myles • *Odyssey Calling*, Vahni Capildeo • *The Long Week-End*, Wilfred Bion • *Confessions of an English Opium-Eater*, Thomas De Quincey • 'If', Rudyard Kipling • *The Wanderer* • 'My Boy Jack', Rudyard Kipling • Acts 15:18, King James Bible • Ecclesiasticus 44:14, King James Bible

ACKNOWLEDGEMENTS

Enormous thanks to the editors of publications in which earlier versions of some of these poems appeared: *Blackbox Manifold*, *Butcher's Dog*, *Gloam*, *Carcanet New Poetries VIII*, *PN Review*, *The Rialto* and *Tentacular*. Thanks to Grace Linden for her wonderful *Project Self-Detective*, for which I wrote 'Micro'. 'Brighton Poppies' was written over biscuits and discussion at Cardinal Newman Catholic School's poetry club and first published in its zine, *Biscuit Poems*. Thanks to my students for their inspirational brilliance.

Love to the most amazing readers and critics, whose input has been the making of *Poppy*: Will Harris, Hugh Foley, Isabella Hammad and Zaffar Kunial, and thanks to John McAuliffe for immaculate editorial input. Love to Kabe Wilson for electrifying emails and for the stunning painting that graces the cover. Love to James Burton, Natasha Allden, Dolly Rae Star, Verity Spott and Kat Addis for constituting the most actualising, phantasmic supergroup in the history of Woodvale cemetery, and to Verity and Ben Graham for their night Horseplay, where I first read some of these poems. Love to Dante Traynor, Gamaliel Traynor, David Noble and Matthew Barnes for our ongoing, magical experiment in bringing poetry and improvisation together. Love to my mum, Mary Chadwick, my dad, Michael Minden, Jason Todd and Ruth Borthwick for decades of guidance, conversation and inspiration. And of all the love most love of all to Kat Addis for everything.